I believe that peace
begins in your mind,
in your heart, and
lives all around you.
Remember, peace is on
your lips and in your
hands.

ANTOINETTE SAMPSON

I remember...

when I came here

Peace
Angels

Antoinette Sampson

WARNER BOOKS

An AOL Time Warner Company

To Emma, Julian, Isabella, Christian, Sam, Sophie, Harrison, Amy, Christopher, Lucienne, Maximilian, Hamish, Joshua, Claudia, Brianna, Jessica, Alexander, Rian, Beatrice & Camilla.

This Warner Books edition is published by arrangement with Random House Australia Pty. Ltd., 20 Alfred Street, Milsons Point NSW 2061

Originally published in Australia

Warner Books, Inc., 1271 Avenue of the Americas, New York, NY 10020

Visit our Web site at www.twbookmark.com.

 An AOL Time Warner Company

Printed in the United States of America

First Warner Books Printing: October 2002
9 8 7 6 5 4 3 2 1

ISBN: 0-446-53159-6
Library of Congress Control Number: 2002106793

Creator & Artistic Director: Antoinette Sampson
Text: Rob Sampson
Photographers: Emma Blaxland, Damien Pleming
Additional Photography: Craig Cranko, John Fryz, Steve Burgess
Design: Greendot Design

The Peace Angels is a registered trademark.

The Peace Angels®

www.peaceangelsonline.com

The Peace Angels gratefully acknowledges the support and assistance of: Olivia Bonnici, Krista Cassidy, Bianca Chiminello, Linen Chol, Dean Clyke, Alex O'Loughlin, Joni Pollard, Bonnee Robinson, Raymond Rusli, Niki Sernak, Shamila Wickramage, Zigi Howes, Christopher Thomas, Nicole Fantl, Isabella Noall, Emma Blaxland, Milan Keyser, Margaret Schuthof, Ellen Schuthof, Liandra Munene, Rohan Mackellar, Jade Evans, Camilla Vincent, Maggie Ireland, Lucienne Ireland, Emma Jacobs, Jack Taylor, Jordan Southern, Àli Gutteridge, Beatrice Vincent, Tara Borrelli, Christian Sampson, Christopher Ireland, Eric Borrelli, Jim O'Connor, Louise Pleming, Sophie Haydon, Lina Corrigan, Kartini Saddington, Ian Bryant, Josiane Bryant, Kathleen Schuthof, Matthew Schuthof, Marcel Schuthof, Lara Bryant, Aidan Bryant, Sean Barclay, Tse-Yee Teh, Tom Robertson, Trilby Beresford, Jack Wardana, Yula George, Brother Anthony, Isabella Sampson, Michael Ho, Kyron Ho, Mark Howath, John Stephen Butterworth, Anthony Carroll, Thomas Carroll, Amy Ireland, Socratis Otto, Yudhi Srinivasan, Emma Rusher, Annie Colthard, Bella Vendramini, Jessica Love, Fiona Love, Saemi Baba, Anne Castle, Rosemary Reid, Maddy Alexander, Sophia Alexander, Alex Threlfall, Venus Morcos, Lorna Black, Posie Graeme-Evans, Lydia Alexander, Betty Williams, Antoinette Wilson, Angela Alegounarias, Julie Burland, Madeleine Van Leer, Roland Hoog, Kathryn Cooper, Ilaine Navea, Wendy Shotton, L. M. Colclough, Lesley-Anne Becker, Michelle Booth, Danny Vendramini, Emma Jade, Ann Tye, Bronwen Jones, Carel Filmer, Betty Filmer, Maggie Hamilton, Doris Nuares, Blake Read, Eloise Haydon, Cinnamon Pollard, Jenny Campbell, Frank Flynn, Scott Lewin, Olivia De Vere, Melina Gissing, Jean Paul Rodriguzz, Jared Kruizinge, Nancy Wood, Cate Shore, Christine Giorgio, Vera Pavlavich, Aimee Jones, Christian Draxl, Melissa Holroyd, Callan Francis Mulvey, Lara Cox, Harrison Haydon, Husein Bristina, Josef Reif, Narelle Green, Phillip Bond, David Reid, Sam Haydon, Helga Pike, Brandon Blythe, Jamie Vertucci, Isabelle Vertucci, Hazel Rex, Dan Potra, Steve Bull, Samuel Lam, Jason Jessup, Dav Evans, Val Holland, Richard Chappel, David John Ruffolo, James Haydon, Max Sernack, Ruben Blundell, Robin Monkhouse, Caitlin Moore, Billy Hughes-Tweedie, Betty Blomfield, Ernie Blomfield, Rosemary Butterworth, Robert Smith, Marelle Mc Colm, Jeannette Sharpe, Graheme Doherty, Kerry Noall, Carmel Niland, Greta Fahlstrom, Val Friss, Anthony Mclellan, Linley Casey, Matthew Casey, Liam Casey, Sheila Drummond, Toni Reiseger, Paul Dravet, Ryan Bishell, Gabriela Tyslova, Rory Unite, Faith Martin, Daniel Sullivan, Reuben Blundell, Camilla Franks, Sri Sathya Sai Baba, Sananda.

St. Andrews Anglican Church (Roseville), Hayden Orpheum Picture Palace, Newtown Performing Arts High School, Pioneer Studios, Bar Italia, Mint Bar, St Josephs College, Hunters Hill, The National Institute of Dramatic Art (Nida), Rosedale Riding Equestrian Centre, Fitzroy Falls, The Coffee Bean, The Southern Cross Academy of Light, Castle Cove Convenience Store, Pittwater Private Hospital, Sydney Kingsford Smith Airport, Paddy's Markets, Market City, Double Bay Bridge Club and the State Rail Authority.

the landing was very

soft

I remember you
were there with me

I opened my eyes

It was a long journey and this was a new place

but it was ok because I was not alone –

you were there.

I always saw you, you and your

friends

shapes and blurs of light and warmth.

I giggled and
spun with the
newness

I was giddy with the

light

I could climb mountains

I could fly

I was a *King*

Where did you go ?

I remember feeling

heavy

the day I went to sleep

I remember...
what do I
remember?

You know
the feeling

not sad or *happy*

sort of in the middle of nothing.

They told me you only
existed in books

that real people
knew better

than

to

believe in

fantasy

And I
believed them

I forgot
you

I remember yearning

the d r e a m s
I had

the sleep-wake existence

I'm just a little tired.

I was feeling

EMPTY

I don't know why

waiting for you to

show

yourself

to remind me that you are here

always

So I searched

I looked for you at the movies...

on the television...

in magazines and on walls... everywhere

but I could not find you.

Memory is strong like a computer chip.

We are all computers who hold

the memory banks of the universe

and if you *search*

you will find

of something greater than this.

And that is where I *found* you

laughing and smiling

playing peek-a-boo.

Oh I missed you so much.

But I was always here, I
never went away.

Who made the slippery rocks dry...

who made the waves

softer

who stopped that car...

who made you jump so *high*

who washed away the fever...

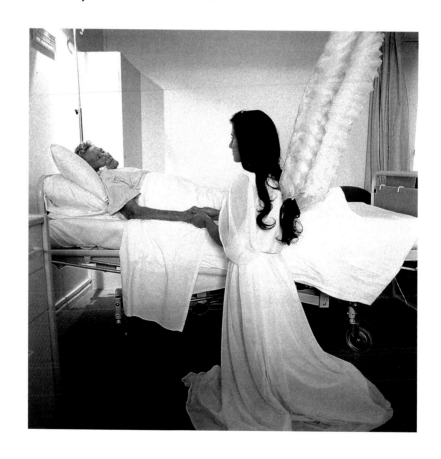

who
loved
you to life?

you are
never *alone*

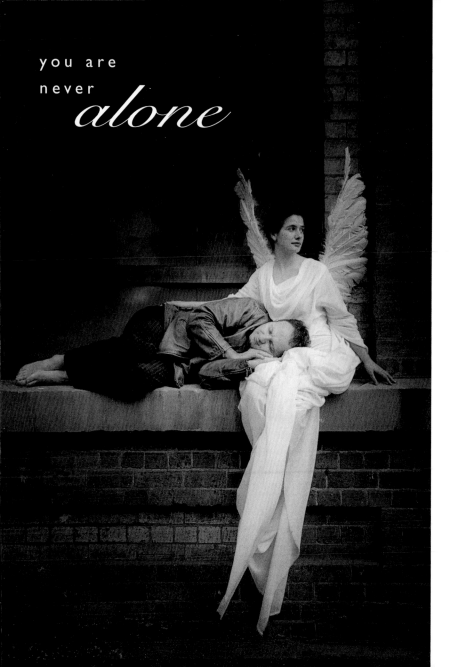

Take steps,
make decisions

don't be afraid.

Remember who you are

the one you see in your dreams

the one you love

the one you forgive.

For when you look into my eyes

you *see*

yourself.

You see

I have never left you

I will never *leave*

you

we are together always

every *breath*

until the last.

And when you leave

on another adventure.

You are good

company

I like being around

you

Take me with you